This edition printed in 2018
by Carlton Books Limited
20 Mortimer Street
London W1T 3JW

A CIP catalogue record for this book is
available from the British Library

ISBN 978-1-78739-044-7

Editorial Director: Martin Corteel
Design Manager: Luke Griffin
Designer: James Pople
Picture Research: Paul Langan
Production: Lisa Cook

Printed in Dubai

ANTHONY
JOSHUA

PORTRAIT OF A BOXING HERO

IAIN SPRAGG

CARLTON
BOOKS

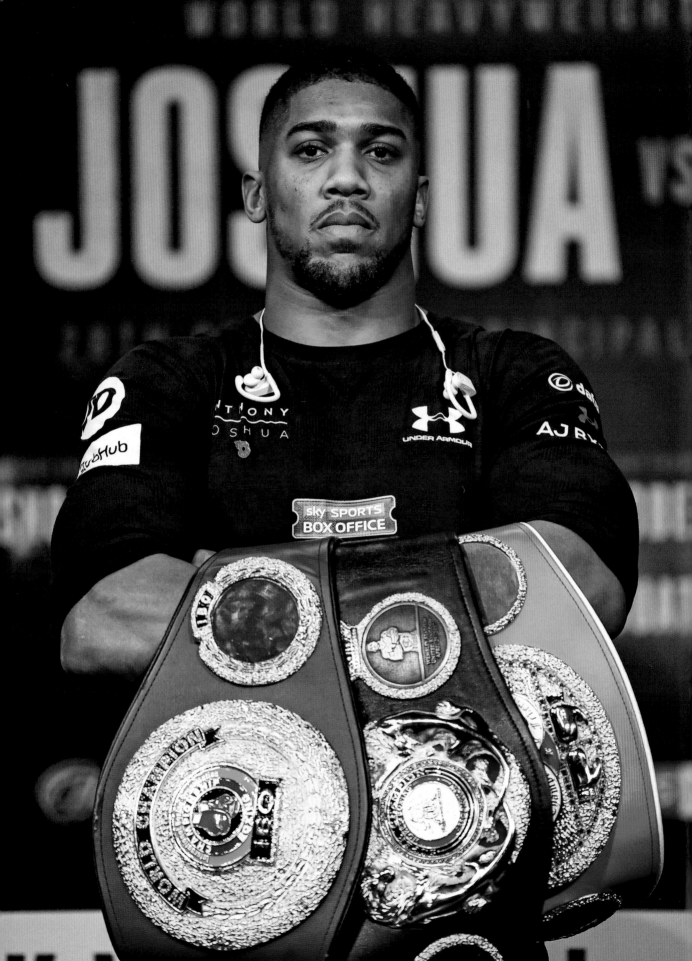

CONTENTS

CHAMPION OF THE WORLD   8

1   THE EARLY YEARS   12

2   AMATEUR CHAMPION   20

3   OLYMPIC GLORY   32

4   WEIGHING THE OPTIONS   46

5   STEPPING INTO THE UNKNOWN   58

6   RISING THROUGH THE RANKS   74

7   WORLD CHAMPION   90

8   EPIC KLITSCHKO BATTLE   104

9   DEFENDING HIS CROWN   118

10   WHAT NEXT FOR AJ?   138

CAREER STATISTICS   148

PICTURE CREDITS   160

Sport is nothing without superstars and in Anthony Oluwafemi Olaseni Joshua, boxing has unearthed one of the most explosive and charismatic fighters of any generation ever to grace the ring

British boxing has never been in ruder health. With seven reigning world champions at the end of 2017, the sport is enjoying a remarkable renaissance. But the undisputed jewel in the crown is Anthony Joshua, the man who has singlehandedly reignited an ailing global heavyweight division.

The ring's biggest and strongest exponents have always been boxing's marquee brand, but the division had become tired and predictable. Then AJ detonated onto the scene. After famously winning gold at the 2012 Summer Olympics in London, he decided to join the professional ranks and began rewriting the sport's record books. Joshua has now put heavyweight boxing back on the map.

At six foot six and weighing around 18 stone, he has a raw power coupled with a technical ability that belies his relatively late introduction to the sport, and which has seen him fight all challengers into submission in his still fledgling career. Few so far have been able to match his natural athleticism, speed and technique – and none have been able to find any answers to his sheer brute force.

His rise to greatness has been as meteoric as it has been merciless. His first pro fight came in late 2013 when he was just 24, and in less than three years he celebrated his first world belt after a trademark knockout of America's Charles Martin for the vacant IBF heavyweight title. AJ had reached the pinnacle of global boxing after only 16 outings.

That triumph was merely the appetizer. He has never made a secret of his ambition to become the undisputed world champion, and in 2017 he took another huge step towards making his dream a reality when he faced Wladimir Klitschko at Wembley.

Joshua had never before stepped into the ring with a man of the Ukrainian's quality. It was the chance of a lifetime, and AJ decisively seized it with both of his sizeable fists. After an epic 11-round battle, he added the WBA and IBO heavyweight belts to his burgeoning collection.

His spectacular victory propelled him into the sporting stratosphere and there are few more popular or famous athletes in the world today. Joshua has already transcended both boxing and his nationality and the only point of debate is exactly how much he can achieve in the ring.

His story is one of success in the face of childhood challenges. He was born in Watford in 1989 to Nigerian parents, and his brushes with the law suggested that the teenager would only ever make headlines for the wrong reasons. Family and fate intervened, however, to ensure his life took a dramatic, unexpected turn.

Finchley Amateur Boxing Club in north London was the scene for his Road to Damascus moment. Joshua was 18 when his cousin took him to the club – and from the moment he first pulled on a pair of gloves, he felt an immediate affinity with the sport. A new path now lay ahead of him.

AJ's first fight was held in late 2008 and within a year he had claimed his first tournament victory. Further amateur accolades quickly followed, but it was his Olympic displays in the ExCeL in east London in 2012 that propelled his career to a new level. From the moment he stood on the podium proudly clutching his gold medal after dethroning the defending champion Roberto Cammarelle, Britain had a new sporting icon.

The post-Games clamour for Joshua to go full time was loud and long, and ultimately proved irresistible. He signed for the renowned Matchroom Sport stable and rapidly built a reputation as one of the most fearsome and ferocious fighters on the circuit. It was simply impossible to ignore the youngster as yet another opponent was left crumpled on the canvas.

His first outing as a professional lasted less than three minutes. Subsequently, challenger after challenger was conclusively stopped in his tracks by Joshua's destructive punching power. Only one of his first ten fights went beyond the second round.

Blessed with an unerring work ethic, a humility born out of a tough background and all the athletic attributes a heavyweight could wish for, AJ now has history in his sights: he wants to become the first man ever to hold all five top weight world belts concurrently.

Only time will tell whether he is successful in his pursuit of all five, but Watford's favourite son can already be legitimately talked about in the same breath as some of boxing's all-time greats. His victory over Martin in 2013 to claim the IBF title made him only the fourth heavyweight in history to win a world title as the reigning Olympic champion. Those to have previously achieved the feat are the legends Floyd Patterson, Muhammad Ali and Leon Spinks. Joshua was also the first British boxer to hold the two coveted titles at the same time.

Boxing is undoubtedly an unforgiving sport, but it is also a form of show business – and AJ has proved to be pure box office. His showdown with Klitschko was broadcast live in more than 150 countries worldwide, and it broke the British record for pay-per-view subscriptions, set two years previously by Floyd Mayweather against Manny Pacquiao in America. Fight fans want to watch him because they know they'll be entertained while a legion of new supporters have been drawn to the sport by his huge personality and dynamic performances.

Joshua's career has already been a thrilling, rollercoaster ride but it seems certain there is so much more to come. The triple world champion will not turn 30 until late 2019 and with heavyweights renowned for their longevity, his best is surely yet to come. AJ is a man who has the world at his feet and a decade of unprecedented dominance in the division within his grasp.

1 **THE EARLY** YEARS

Childhood upheaval and trouble with the police proved the making of AJ as he transformed himself from troubled teenager into a future world champion

There is a common theme in poetry and literature of inner strength forged in the crucible of adversity. In the case of Anthony Joshua, it's undoubtedly true that he would not be the fighter or man he is today were it not for his experiences in the first, sometimes chaotic 20 years of his life.

He is the son of Nigerian immigrants Yeta and Robert, who arrived in the UK in their early twenties, and he grew up on the Meriden Estate in the Watford suburb of Garston. At the age of five, his parents split up, and AJ and his three siblings were raised by their mother.

In 2002 his domestic situation changed dramatically when Yeta relocated the family to Nigeria and enrolled her then 11-year-old son at a boarding school. By his own admission it was a complete shock to his system – but while the school's regime was strict, he admits it wasn't all negative.

"I thought I was going to Nigeria on holiday. I wasn't prepared for it. At the time you think 'Why?', but as you get older you think it was good that you experienced it. We stayed out there, not long, only six months. [We started at] 5.30 in the morning: up, fetch your water. Your clothes had to be washed and ironed. We got beaten. That's my culture, beating."

He returned to England aged 12 and started at the Kings Langley School near Watford in Hertfordshire. It was here, in secondary education, that his natural athletic prowess, as well as his teenage tendency for trouble, began to emerge.

In Year Nine Joshua ran a phenomenal 11.6 seconds for the 100 metres and also played centre forward for the school football team. He was a gifted footballer, but his competitive edge led to problems: in one match the 16-year-old manhandled an opposition player by the neck and flung him onto the pitch, an act that resulted in a charge of Actual Bodily Harm (ABH).

"I was quite a good striker at school, but during one game this guy was trying to wind me up," he said. "I got him round the neck and threw him

over my shoulder. I didn't know my own strength and he didn't land too well. Incredibly, it went to court and I was charged with ABH. Luckily, they ended up giving me a slap across the wrist."

Sadly, further dealings with the judicial system were to follow. He left school at 16 and divided his time between sleeping in a series of hostels in Watford and staying with Yeta at the new family home in Golders Green, north London. The constant upheaval led, perhaps inevitably, to problems. After a late-night fracas in 2009, he was arrested and put on remand in Reading prison, for what he has subsequently described as "fighting and other crazy stuff".

His temporary detention terrified AJ to such an extent that he bought a set of weights in order to bulk up his muscles in readiness for the threats of violence which he believed would accompany a custodial sentence. In the end he was conditionally discharged, but the experience left a deep impression on the youngster.

"I was on remand in Reading for two weeks. There are idiots inside, and this is when you realize what you are dealing with in prison. Once you're there, it's fifty-fifty, because you've been found guilty, so I was preparing myself for the worst. It could have been 10 years."

After his release, Joshua moved back in with Yeta. He started work as a bricklayer, but it was his cousin Ben Ileyemi who was the most instrumental in helping him to start to turn his life around.

Salvation came in the shape of the Finchley Amateur Boxing Club.

ABOVE: AJ, father Robert (left) and aunt Cheryl (right) celebrate after his seventh round knockout of fellow Brit Dillian Whyte at the O2 Arena in December 2015.

"" My guardian angel decided I didn't need to be punished with a jail sentence. But I was on tag for over a year, and that helped. I became so disciplined when I was on tag. I would be at home by eight o'clock and because I had boxing, I lived the disciplined life. I started reading because I learned that so many champions educated themselves. Joe Louis, Mike Tyson, Bernard Hopkins. Before it was 'Act now, think later', but the discipline and reading changed me. ""

ANTHONY JOSHUA on his 2008 custodial reprieve

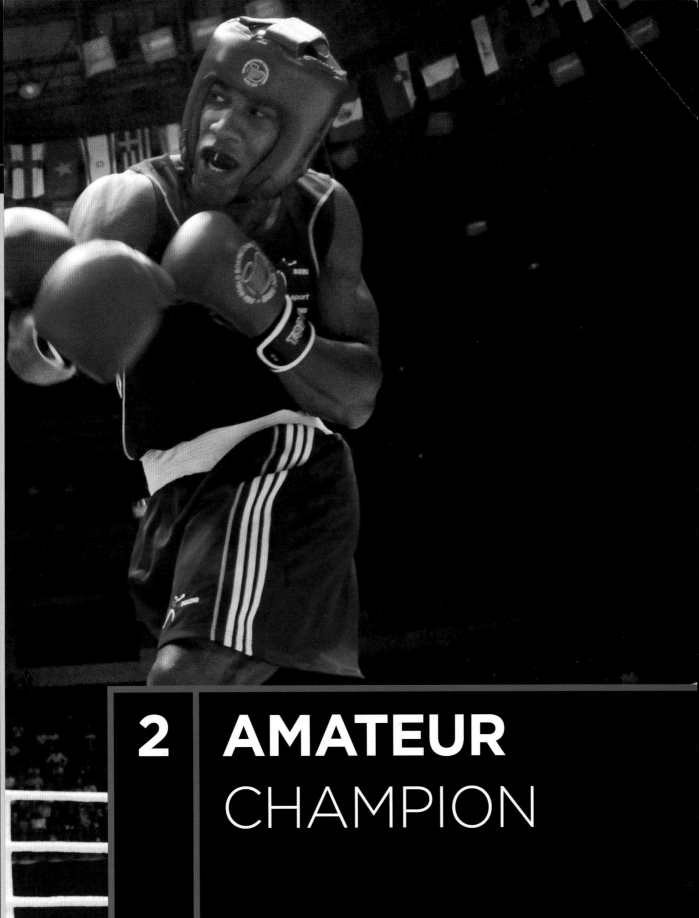

2 AMATEUR
CHAMPION

ABOVE: Joshua's powerful displays for GB Boxing during the AIBA World Boxing Championships in Azerbaijan in 2011 announced the arrival of the youngster on the global stage.

The win was significant for two reasons. Firstly, it meant AJ had now joined an exclusive cast list. ABA super-heavyweight champions of previous years include Audley Harrison, fellow Finchley graduate Dereck Chisora, David Price and Tyson Fury – all of whom went on to win Olympic and Commonwealth Games medals and, in the case of Fury, the world heavyweight title.

Secondly, his success attracted the attention of promoters. In the wake of his victory over Winrow, the teenager was offered £50,000 to join the professional ranks. Relinquishing his amateur status at such a young age was not part of the master plan, though, and although he did agonize, he eventually rejected the approach.

"I didn't take up the sport for money, I wanted to win medals. Not turning pro when I was younger is the biggest decision I've made. People were advising me to do certain things, but I followed my gut. You follow your gut and hope it works. The iron was hot, so do I do a deal or do I turn it down and maybe go out at the weekend on a motorbike and break my hand?"

Mercifully both his hands remained unscathed, and later in 2010 he added another belt to his burgeoning collection when he beat Amin Isa to become the Great Britain champion. AJ's elevation from unknown hopeful to the status of a bona fides prospect was gathering pace, and in 2011 he applied his foot to the career accelerator.

It was the busiest year of his career to date. Outside the ring he was dealing with the ongoing legal repercussions of his drugs arrest. When his GB Boxing suspension was eventually lifted, he set about making up for lost time.

His first major assignment came in May, when he defended his ABA super-heavyweight title at Charter Hall in Colchester. He faced Fayz Abbas in the final and although the eventual 24:15 points decision went in his favour, it was a rusty performance lacking sparkle – which spoke volumes about the turbulence of previous months.

"There's a lot more to come," he admitted after the fight. "I cannot blame my opponent for how I boxed, and that was not the real Anthony Joshua in there. This wasn't my best performance, you cannot judge me on that. I'm learning so much every time I fight. The World Championships is the big one this year and I just hope they have me written down as Number 1 on their notepad. I'm taking it one step at a time, I got this fight out the way, and now I'll turn my attention to the next thing. I'll be back in the gym on Monday. There is so much more to come, though. Boxing is my future."

Selection for the European rather than World Championships was, however, Joshua's more pressing concern in the wake of his second ABA triumph. It was not until the eleventh hour that GB Boxing made contact to confirm he was going to Turkey for the tournament. The late notice afforded him just three weeks' worth of training and he headed to Ankara for the biggest competition of his career in far from ideal shape.

It was to his credit that he was able to despatch both Eric Brechlin of Germany and Northern Ireland's Cathal McMonagle in the early rounds, but he was stopped by Romanian southpaw Mihai Nistor in the quarter-finals to end his medal hopes. Nistor remains the only fighter ever to have stopped Joshua in either the amateur or professional ranks.

The Romanian national champion came at Joshua relentlessly from the first bell. His aggressive, agricultural style unsettled his opponent, but it was not until the third round that the southpaw made meaningful contact, catching AJ with two swinging shots with his left. Neither rocked him unduly, but after his second standing count, the referee decided the fight was over. The look on AJ's face, a mixture of disgust and disbelief, told the audience exactly what he thought of the decision.

There was, though, a silver lining to the Ankara cloud. GB Boxing decided that AJ had done enough to earn his place in the team to compete in the upcoming World Championships in Azerbaijan, and for this he would now have the luxury of time to prepare. The stage was set for Joshua's first appearance on a global stage.

In truth, he jetted out to Heydar Aliyev Sports and Exhibition Complex in Baku in October as a quantity unknown to the vast majority of his rival super-heavyweights. News of his exploits in Britain had not yet reached further afield, his name was not high on anyone's list of pre-tournament contenders and he was certainly not among the Top 10 seeds going into the competition. AJ was supposed to be there first and foremost to gain valuable international experience.

His first three fights – against Tariq Abdul-Haqq of Trinidad and Tobago, Juan Isidro Hiracheta of Mexico and Mohamed Arjaoui of Morocco – all went AJ's way, but his quarter-final opponent was the renowned Roberto Cammarelle, the Italian two-time world champion, reigning Olympic gold medallist (from Beijing 2008) and the boxer ranked No. 1 in the tournament. Joshua had surely met his match.

The fight initially went according to the preordained script, Cammarelle dominating the first round. Then a left uppercut in the second and long right in the third from the younger man rocked the Italian. It was down to the judges to separate the pair, and they came back with a 15-13 decision to Joshua. The youngster had never overcome a fighter with such a pedigree.

"I always believed I could beat Cammarelle, so I'm not shocked about the result," he said. "It's not always the name but who is the best boxer on the day. Cammarelle is a legend and I have great respect for him."

The semi-final against Germany's Erik Pfeifer was a shorter and altogether more brutal affair. Joshua caught his opponent with a booming punch in the first round, and as blood flowed from Pfeifer's nose, the referee had no option but to call a premature halt to proceedings.

His foe in the final was Azerbaijan's Mahommedrasul Majidov, fighting in front of a partisan home crowd. The ensuing battle between the World No. 2 and the 21-year-Englishman proved to be epic. Joshua's jab gave him the ascendency in the first round, but as the bout unfolded, Majidov rallied and the fight became more of a brawl. AJ had to take a standing count in the second, and as the pair continued to go toe to toe, there was nothing to choose between them. When the bell sounded at the end of the third, the result remained in doubt. The judges deliberated and finally decided Majidov had edged it by the narrowest of margins, awarding the fight 22:21 to the Azerbaijani.

"I'm so disappointed," Joshua said after collecting his silver medal. "One hundred per cent I'm disappointed, I wanted to get the gold. You just asking me now, it hurts, man, it hurts. It's always one fight at a time, but we'd prepared well for the World Championships."

ABOVE: Joshua's growing profile after the World Championships was underlined when he was invited to attend the Aviva and *Daily Telegraph* School Sport Matters Awards at Twickenham.

His disappointment was palpable, but while he was contemplating what might have been, others in Baku had watched his fights and come to rather different conclusions about his performances and what the future held.

"Joshua's emergence here has been a revelation," wrote the respected boxing journalist Gareth A. Davies in the *Daily Telegraph*. "The Finchley boxer, who turns 22 next week, stopped Pfeifer in the opening round of the semi-final, the referee unhappy about the blood pouring from the

> **❝ Losing to Majidov was a tough fight. But I knew I had to fight to the end, until that final bell. I know that if I keep on fighting, right until that bell, I'm going be fine. That's how I get through. ❞**

AJ on being denied gold

FOLLOWING PAGES:
AJ listens intently to the speeches at the Aviva and *Daily Telegraph* School Awards at Twickenham Stadium.

German's nose. Joshua had already shown in the opening two minutes that he possesses poise, power and movement, and his booming shots looked to have broken Pfeifer's nose.

"It has been a remarkable tournament for Joshua, signalled notably with a win over Roberto Cammarelle, the Olympic and two-time world champion, at the quarter-final stage. After those nine minutes, Joshua became a commodity whose stock will rise as far as the professional ranks after next year's London Games. A massive learning curve for Joshua. A star is born."

Prophetic words indeed – and ones with which Davies's press colleagues evidently agreed. The Boxing Writers Club of Great Britain named AJ as their Amateur Boxer of the Year for 2011. Less than three years after his maiden fight, the boy from Watford was beginning to make serious waves.

More welcome recognition was quick to follow when he was invited to live and train four days a week with the rest of the GB squad at the English Institute of Sport in Sheffield. His victory over Cammarelle in the last eight in Azerbaijan had booked his place at the 2012 Olympics in London, and GB Boxing were keen to bring their embryonic star firmly into the fold. In 10 months' time he would repay the faith shown in him in truly spectacular style.

Only one British boxer had ever claimed super-heavyweight gold at the Games previously – Audley Harrison in Sydney in 2000 – and AJ was now on the path to emulating his achievement.

" Straightaway you could see all his physical advantages, but there was something about him too. A presence. In the ring, he was tall and rangy, and it was all about harnessing his attributes and steering him. AJ soaked up anything we could teach him. He was very dedicated – first in, last out. He was stimulated by it all and soaked up the details we could give him like a sponge. He listened to everyone. "

RICHIE WOODHALL, Team GB technical adviser, on AJ's first appearance at the English Institute of Sport in Sheffield

3 | OLYMPIC
GLORY

With his Team GB place at the 2012 Summer Olympics in London now assured, Joshua set his sights on making his mark on amateur boxing's greatest stage

I t is a rare breed of boxer indeed who is fortunate enough to compete at the Olympics, let alone stand on the podium clutching a medal. The Games are the pinnacle for the amateur ranks of the sport, and over the years some of Britain's most iconic fighters – from Henry Cooper to Amir Khan, Alan Minter to James DeGale – have represented the country with distinction at the Games.

Joshua joined their ranks courtesy of his quarter-final victory over Roberto Cammarelle in Azerbaijan in 2011, but with less than a year in which to prepare for the biggest challenge of his career so far, there was no time to waste. The youngster needed to be in the best shape of his life. With his personal problems well and truly behind him, he worked tirelessly with the Team GB coaching staff in Sheffield.

He would go on to do Britain proud, but a fascinating footnote in the Joshua story is the intriguing if unconfirmed report that he could potentially have boxed for Nigeria, his parents' home country, at the 2008 Summer Olympics in Beijing.

The man himself has never commented on the rumour, but it seems that the youngster's Olympic career could have unfolded rather differently. At least, that's the story from Obisia Nwankpa, the former Commonwealth light welterweight champion between 1979 and 1983 and the head coach of the Nigerian national team at the time.

"He reached out to us, asking to be part of our Olympic team [in 2008]. So we invited him to come down and take part in trials. Unfortunately he did not appear when we asked him to and came down only when we had finished our trials, finalized our team and were about to travel for a training tour. Maybe other coaches would have accepted it, but I could not. It's a pity he did not get his chance at that time, but the two boxers we selected then were outstanding and experienced and there was no way I was going to drop them for somebody I had not even seen."

Whatever the truth, AJ did not box for Nigeria in 2008 and their loss was to be Britain's glorious gain. In the build-up to the London Games, there was absolutely no doubting exactly where his allegiance lay.

"I'm very proud to represent Britain," he said. "If you win an Olympic gold, you are never a former Olympian. As a professional, as a heavyweight champion, once you lose the belts you are a former heavyweight champion. But you are always an Olympian, you can't take that away. Boxing at the Olympics is on my mind every day. I want to get the gold medal at those Olympics."

The comparisons between AJ and Audley Harrison, the super-heavyweight champion in Sydney 12 years earlier, were perhaps inevitable as the Games approached, and Joshua readily acknowledged the impact Harrison had made on the domestic amateur ranks.

"A lot of people have got bad things to say about him but at the same time, for British boxing, he opened up so many gates. He was an ABA champion, a Commonwealth champion, so as an amateur you've got to remember what he did. I know he didn't do too well as a pro, but from an amateur stance, he's an Olympic champion as a boxer and he is British."

Joshua's selection for the Games would have a pivotal effect on his subsequent career in more ways than one – not least because it brought him into regular contact with Rob McCracken. Team GB's head coach would help steer the youngster through his Olympic odyssey and, in recent

BELOW: Joshua took time out from his Olympic preparations to spar with Hollywood actor Will Smith, the star of the 2001 Muhammad Ali biopic.

OPPOSITE: AJ was aiming to become only the second British boxer, after Audley Harrison at Sydney 2000, to be crowned Olympic super-heavyweight champion.

years, the perils and pitfalls of the professional ranks. In 2012, however, the former Commonwealth middleweight champion was focused solely on ensuring AJ was ready for London.

"We always knew we had something special on our hands with Anthony, but his rate of progress this year, for someone who is still relatively inexperienced, has been absolutely fantastic," McCracken said. "As long as he continues to work hard in the gym, listen to the coaches and develop as a boxer, then he has every chance of being a star in his hometown Olympics."

By the time the boxing events at the Games finally arrived in August 2012, Joshua stood fourth in the world rankings. Fifteen of the sport's finest amateur super-heavyweights were waiting for him, however, and even with a vociferous, partisan home crowd cheering him on inside the ExCeL, the jury was still out. Did he really have what it takes to secure a medal?

OUR GREATEST TEAM
TEAM GB
TEAM GB
adidas
TEAM GB
London 2012

roared, Joshua stepped up his work rate, and courtesy of the judge's 13-11 decision in his favour, he was through to the final.

"I have just got to stay calm," he told reporters after the fight. "That's all I keep telling myself. I'm still a day away from gold. It is not just about me. I know I have got my family at home, my coaches at Finchley ABC, the friends up there and everyone buzzing. It's a team achievement and I am just happy I can make everyone smile."

His date with destiny was 12 August 2012 and his rival for the title a familiar one: Roberto Cammarelle, the reigning Olympic champion and the man he had beaten in the quarter-finals of the World Championships a year earlier. The Italian did not let the word revenge pass his lips in the build-up to the fight, but there was no doubt Cammarelle felt, at least

privately, that he had a point to prove. "He deserved to beat me in the world championships," he said. "This time I will beat him."

There were many who believed him. The Italian had the pedigree, after all, and he had proved his class in his own semi-final, beating on points the world champion Mahommedrasul Majidov, who had overcome Joshua in Baku 10 months earlier. As befitted a final, the fight would be AJ's greatest challenge yet.

A certain Wladimir Klitschko was in the audience at the ExCeL to witness proceedings. The Ukrainian had won Olympic gold at the Atlanta Games in 1996, and the reigning WBO and WBC world heavyweight champion now sat down to watch the nine minutes that would decide the 2012 champion. It was time for the action.

The first of the three rounds saw the home favourite make light of the magnitude of the occasion with a series of penetrating jabs, but his concentration lapsed in the final seconds of the opener and he was caught in the corner. Cammarelle's late burst allowed the Italian to steal the round 6-5.

Joshua rallied in the second with another series of successful jabs, but Cammarelle was nonetheless getting through with punches of his own. The juddering left hook from Joshua was undeniably the shot of the round, but the Italian edged it with the judges and took the second 7-5.

The Brit was trailing 13-10 heading into the final three minutes, and it seemed that his challenge would come up agonizingly short. The last two minutes, though, saw Joshua display unerring accuracy just when it really mattered. Landing a rapid succession of shots, he dramatically levelled the scores at 18 each at the bell.

"Joshua, who was under pressure at the end of the first round and at the start of the second, found composure in a hurricane," wrote Kevin Mitchell in *The Guardian*. "Cammarelle, a Milanese policeman, has been a fine champion for a long time and briefly seemed on the verge of overwhelming an opponent who had had only 43 amateur bouts, losing three.

"The scores were level at 18-18 after nine minutes and went to countback – incorporating the scores of all five judges rather than just the median three – and Joshua had edged it by three points. That was not convincing enough for the Italians, who appealed. When the result of the short hearing was confirmed, the capacity audience, not for the first time over the past fortnight, filled the hall with the most heartfelt roar."

It was a shattering denouement to the Games for the Italian and his disappointment was palpable.

"I still don't know why – even with the same score – I was the one to lose," he said in the wake of defeat. "I thought they would see that I was superior in the fight. In Baku [last year] versus Joshua, I didn't lose. In Ankara, in the European Championship final against a Russian boxer, I did not lose. It's now been three years that I feel that the judges are against me. I don't know if my punch is invisible. I feel tired. I want to go home. Maybe I want to cry."

The emotions experienced by Joshua were in sharp contrast, of course. As he began to come to terms with being the new Olympic champion, the 22-year-old from Watford was already being talked about in boxing circles as a potential future world champion.

AJ, himself, was happy to leave that talk to others. Standing proudly on the podium, with the national anthem playing, he was content just to revel in what he had just achieved.

"Sunday is a holy day and I have been blessed. There are no easy fights in these Olympics. I have pulled it out of the bag and my heart is pumping with adrenaline. That medal represents my journey and the support from my team. It is much more than a gold medal, it is a life experience.

"I'm a warrior and I needed a big last round to get this medal round my neck, and I had it. This is a medal for everybody that has ever helped me and for everybody to start their own dream. I have had to overcome a lot of obstacles, but I never stopped dreaming of the Olympic medal. I played it over and over in my mind. It was a close fight and it has made me realize I need more experience at the top level."

It would not be until the following year that he finally decided whether his education would be furthered in the amateur or professional ranks. This would be perhaps the most difficult decision of his sporting life, but what was clear was that Joshua had now become one of boxing's biggest draws.

BELOW: The final against defending Olympic champion Roberto Cammarelle was a repeat of AJ's quarter-final defeat of the Italian at the 2011 AIBA World Boxing Championships.

FOLLOWING PAGES: Gold medal around his neck and draped in the Union Jack, AJ celebrates becoming the London 2012 Olympic champion.

" I was in serious pain, but I just won't ever give up in there. I will keep pushing to the last bell. My legs and everything were killing me, but I just kept throwing punches, catching him with straight shots down the middle. I never panicked. Sometimes I wanted to stop, but my arms were just flying. My job is to do the fighting in the ring. The judges' job is to decide who the winner is. I've had close fights all over the world and I've lost a couple in my short career. I take it on the chin and I move on. "

JOSHUA after he overcame Roberto Cammarelle to win the London 2012 Olympic super-heavyweight gold medal

4 | **WEIGHING** THE OPTIONS

❝ I had two distinct choices: either stay as an amateur and continue to learn and gain experience or turn pro and test the pressures of becoming the British heavyweight sensation and potentially being rushed through my career due to expectations based on my amateur pedigree. It took me almost a year to make the decision, a decision I can never go back on and a decision I feel I will never regret. I'm so determined and so willing to sacrifice anything and everything to achieve my dreams. **❞**

ANTHONY JOSHUA on his decision to embrace professionalism

5 STEPPING INTO THE UNKNOWN

Joshua remained patient despite his opponent's obvious, increasing discomfort. Then, 20 seconds from the end of the first round, he delivered the coup de grâce, unleashing a series of four quick-fire, short-range uppercuts with his right. Leo flailed wildly in a last act of disorientated defiance, but Joshua moved in to finish the job. As the referee rushed in to stop the fight and save Leo from further punishment, the Italian hit the canvas.

"He staggered Leo several times with right crosses and while the Italian marched forward gamely, the effect was rather like watching a World War One soldier walking into a battery of machine-gun fire," wrote Sean Ingle in the *Guardian*. "A series of concussive punches ended it two minutes and 47 seconds into the first round."

Mission accomplished!

By any measure, this had not been a thorough examination of Joshua's professional credentials, but the explosive manner in which he had despatched his opponent so convincingly was nothing if not satisfying. Sterner tests would come, but for now AJ was content to enjoy the victory.

"This was just as important as winning the Olympics. I had been out of the ring for 14 months, but I've built a really strong team around me. It's going to be a tough road and hard work, but I'm going to put the work in. I'd love to be in the heavyweight mix, but I've got a long way to go to get there.

"We'll gauge my progress as I keep winning and keep learning in the gym, and we'll see what I am ready for fight by fight. I don't want to promise things I can't deliver. I don't want to talk much trash. I want to back things up. It's going to be a tough road and hard work, but I'm going to put the work in."

Three weeks later he was back in action on the undercard of Kell Brook's welterweight clash with Ukrainian Vyacheslav Senchenko. The venue was the Motorpoint Arena in the familiar surroundings of Sheffield, and his opponent the vastly experienced Paul Butlin, a British pro of 11 years' standing. At the age of 37, though, he was a fighter in the autumn of his career.

The opening round was a one-sided affair. Once again Joshua's jab looked in fine fettle, and he followed up with a series of muscular blows that rocked Butlin. The veteran had to fall back on all his battle-hardened years of experience to survive – and to ensure that, unlike the Leo fight, a second round was required.

Then, however, AJ needed only a further 50 seconds to bring a brutal end to the proceedings. A left hook saw Butlin's legs betray him, then a crunching straight right smashed through his defences, putting him on the canvas as well as opening up a cut above his left eye. Butlin bravely got to his feet, beating the count, but Joshua showed no mercy and stepped in with a succession of blows that forced the referee to stop the fight. The intervention came just seconds before Butlin's corner threw in the towel.

"He showed so much more composure tonight," said Eddie Hearn. "Butlin is a seasoned pro who went the distance twice with Dereck Chisora. This is a different class we are talking about right here. People talk about we've got to take him at the right pace, but that's going to be very difficult to do."

The brevity of the bout again left questions unanswered about Joshua's technique or his ability to take a decent punch. Butlin, though, was unequivocal: he made it clear that he believed the 24-year-old had more than enough raw power to go all the way.

"I've been in with the biggest lads in Europe. But Joshua's power is horrible. If he hits you, you're gone, simple as that. It's sickening, nobody hits harder than Anthony Joshua. The first jab he hit me with, I went back to the corner shaking my head. He caught me with an overhand right

OPPOSITE: Joshua's
raw power proved
too much for the
Croat Hrvoje Kisicek
and the fight was
stopped by the
referee one minute
and 38 seconds into
the second round.

that gave me nine stitches. How many heavyweights would have got up from the right hand Joshua hit me with? It was a horrible punch, the best I've taken."

With two commanding wins from two, Joshua had done all that could be asked of him. Even so, as he prepared to face Croat Hrvoje Kisicek at the York Hall back in London in November 2013, he admitted that trainer Tony Sims was not exactly getting carried away with his performances so far.

"The only thing I listen to about my prospects is what my coach tells me, and he tells me I'm rubbish and that I've a lot to work on. He tells me I have to keep my feet on the ground, that there are a lot of people out there who are better than me. That is why I need to keep on grafting in the gym. I do appreciate what people are saying about my prospects, but it's early doors. It's one step at a time and I have a long way to go."

Champions past and present, including former world heavyweight champion Larry Holmes and current British and Commonwealth title holder David Price, were ringside to watch Joshua fight in Bethnal Green. Kisicek's record of five wins and six losses was not one to strike fear into his opponent, and with the Croat surrendering a significant height and reach advantage, AJ was the clear favourite.

He did not disappoint the star-studded crowd. From the start he was on the front foot. His jab played the starring role in the first round, but it was a body shot that left the most lasting impression on Kisicek, who winced in pain. When the Croat desperately tried to counter, AJ stepped away from the danger with ease.

The second round was reminiscent of the Butlin fight. Joshua was in no mood for a protracted engagement and visibly upped the ante, catching his opponent with a left-right combination that sent him down. Kisicek took the count and found his feet at eight, but regained the vertical only to be welcomed by a further salvo of bruising shots. The outcome by now was inevitable, and midway through the round the referee Marcus McDonnell stepped in to spare the Croat any more damage. The fight had lasted 48 seconds longer than it took to dispose of Butlin.

"I worked on a few things in there," AJ said. "He was cagey, awkward and durable. It's important to work on things in the gym and take that to the ring. I'll be in Manchester next weekend performing again and I need to be ready for that."

His Manchester assignment was supposed to pit him against Argentina's Hector Alfredo Avila on the undercard of Carl Froch's defence of his WBA and IBF super-middleweight belts against George Groves. Fate had other ideas, though: AJ strained a bicep and on the advice of his medical team he was forced to withdraw. There was further frustrating news in December when a shoulder problem put paid to plans to face Welshman Dorian Darch at the ExCeL.

It was not how he had envisaged finishing 2013, his debut year as a professional. Still, there was the consolation of three muscular wins from three to show for his early efforts, and with the Darch bout rescheduled for February the following year, much to look forward to.

The fight was held at the Motorpoint Arena in Cardiff, and was to be Joshua's first professional foray outside England. Once again, he was expected to put his opponent away without undue alarm, though Darch's record of seven wins in nine outings suggested he might at least be a stubborn opponent. The Welshman, however, was under no illusions.

"I've got my limitations and I know I'm never going to be world champion. I also know Joshua is a huge guy and he's probably going to be too big for me. But you never know, I could hit him on the button and my world can change. It's hard as a heavyweight getting fights in Wales, so I told my manager that I was happy to take some risks. To be fair, he's come up with the Joshua fight and it's a massive opportunity for me."

The crowd in Cardiff was predictably partisan as the two men entered the ring, the majority of the cheers reserved for the Welshman. For most of the opening round, there was faint hope for the locals as Darch avoided his opponent's biggest shots and even caught the Englishman with a rare right hand. That proved a red rag to the bull, and AJ replied with a flurry of punches that was halted only by the bell.

The second round lasted less than a minute. A straight right visibly rocked Darch, and as Joshua moved forward purposefully, referee Terry O'Connor intervened. The Welshman looked poised to fall. It was a fourth straight win, but the first time the Olympic champion had failed to send his opponent to the floor.

"The Olympic gold medallist's seamless transition to the professional ranks continued on Saturday as he knocked out Dorian Darch in just two rounds in Cardiff," reported the *Daily Mail*. "The heavyweight was making his fourth professional outing and extended his 100 per cent record as he put his Welsh opponent down. Out of 24 rounds he could have boxed since joining the paid ranks, the 24-year-old has been in the ring for just seven of them."

AJ himself was unhappy with his performance, and acutely aware that his rise would not continue to be quite so meteoric if he didn't improve. His opponents were only going to get stronger, and he had to be prepared for significantly sterner challenges.

"Not too great tonight. A few things I was noticing in there when I was getting my jab going and my one-two, but you know how it is, the first round you are just warming into the fight. I was trying to capitalize on some of his weaknesses from early on, but as round two came along I started finding my rhythm. The next fight in March, hopefully you will see a bit of improvement."

" I actually started alright. I was making him miss, which isn't something I normally do. I normally just go in there and have a bit of a scrap. For two-and-a-half minutes, I was making him miss and it was all OK. Then he caught me and my head was like a pinball. I didn't go there to lie down, but he was in a different league to me and you could tell that he lives in the gym. He was too good, too big and too strong and I hope he goes on to become a world champion one day. It would be nice to say that you've been beaten by a world champion. "

DORIAN DARCH reflects on his defeat to AJ in Cardiff in 2014

6 RISING THROUGH THE RANKS

RIGHT: AJ took
a break from the
gym in the summer
of 2014 when he
attended Wimbledon
with David Haye,
the former WBA
heavyweight
champion.

OPPOSITE: Joshua's
meteoric rise through
the ranks continued
after an explosive
second round
stoppage of former
British champion
Matt Skelton in
Liverpool in July
2014.

especially when you're in with the new [Mike] Tyson. He hits you through your gloves, even when you've got your hands up protecting your head. The power of his punches goes through your gloves and there's nowhere to hide."

Liverpool's Echo Arena was selected as the venue for AJ's seventh fight in July 2014, facing compatriot Matt Skelton. At the age of 47, Skelton was undoubtedly at the wrong end of his career in the ring, though he had an impressive CV. At various times, he had held the British, Commonwealth and European heavyweight titles.

A former professional kickboxer, Skelton had become British champion a decade earlier when he knocked over Michael Sprott. That particular belt was very much on Joshua's mind as he discussed his upcoming challenge and the strides forward he was making in the professional game.

"I'm ready to take risks, but one step at a time, though, as this is a career. I'm not trying to run a 100-metre sprint. I'm on a marathon now, so next year will be interesting to see where we go, but I've really got to focus on Skelton, who should give me some problems.

"He's someone tall, rangy and a veteran of the sport. I haven't gone past two rounds yet, but it's early days and this is what I should be doing. Hopefully I will get another victory and then I think early next year it will be interesting to see where my management take me heading towards that British title, but what an honour it would be to fight for the British title."

The fight with Skelton on Merseyside initially followed the pattern of his previous outings. AJ established his superiority early on, but as the first round gave way to the second and the clock ticked, there was a growing possibility that Joshua would be taken into a third round for the first time.

" It only went two rounds, but I just wanted to hurt him. I don't like it when the referees step in and stop the fight. He hadn't been stopped, so I just wanted to see what he could take. He was a strong guy and he wasn't an easy opponent, but I wanted to make light work of him. I really enjoyed it. It's time to step it up, that's where the spitefulness is coming in. This is gladiator, the arena. There's a whole ocean of heavyweights out there. **"**

JOSHUA reacts to his victory over Denis Bakhtov to claim the vacant WBC International Heavyweight title

7 | WORLD CHAMPION

clash with Johnson was only 21 days away, though, so this fight was in truth more of a warm-up than meaningful challenge. The bout duly followed the script, Joshua spectacularly stopping his opponent just 1 minute, 21 seconds into the second round, with a fearsome straight right.

The end of the fight was not the end of the entertainment for the audience in Birmingham, however. Johnson climbed into the ring and the two men went face to face before the American threw down a very public gauntlet. "I've got the antidote for this guy," he announced. "I know what I've got to do to stop this guy. This will be the meanest fight anyone has seen."

The boxing world would discover in only three short weeks whether Johnson's bold claim would prove prophetic or foolhardy.

There was little doubt the 35-year-old American had the pedigree to back up his brash confidence. In his 36 professional outings before facing Joshua, he'd won 29 times and drawn once, and had never been stopped in his six losses. He'd fought Vitali Klitschko for the WBC heavyweight title in 2009 and taken the Ukrainian to 12 rounds, and he went the same distance in defeat to Tyson Fury in 2012.

The pre-fight verbal sparring undoubtedly generated an extra edge to the atmosphere inside the O2 Arena, the venue for the clash. The crowd had gleefully installed Johnson as Public Enemy Number 1 and the fans and media alike waited expectantly to see if the Kingpin could justify his bold prediction. "Can Kevin Johnson live up to all those words and take this fella deep?" asked Sky Sports commentator Nick Halling just before the bell. "It's scheduled for 10 rounds, but whether it goes that long remains to be seen."

The first round began cagily and then, after a minute, AJ rocked the American with a brutal right hook. The contest now became one-way traffic, the crowd favourite advancing and Johnson retreating warily. The tactic kept the American out of trouble until 20 seconds before the end of the round, when a close-range onslaught forced him down on one knee and he took the mandatory count. Joshua came again and with another savage assault floored his opponent at the same time as the bell sounded.

Johnson had to be helped back to his corner, and few who saw his slow, unsteady progress to his stool expected him to come out for the second. It was testament to his pride and bravery that he did, but the American barely threw a punch in the second stanza. AJ unloaded time and time again, and just 1 minute, 22 seconds into the round, the referee put him out of his misery.

Joshua's WBC International title was safe and he enjoyed a four-month break from the ring before his next bout. The venue for the September assignment was again the O2 Arena in London. His opponent was Scotland's Gary "Highlander" Cornish and both AJ's WBC crown and the vacant Commonwealth heavyweight belt were on the line.

The clash was notable because it was the first time Joshua had ever stepped into a ring with 12 scheduled rounds ahead of him. Any questions

about his potential stamina over such a distance were left unanswered, though: he required a mere 97 seconds to dispose of his opponent.

Cornish's record of 21 wins in 21, not to mention boasting both the height and weight to rival even AJ, meant that the neutral spectators had been hoping for a prolonged encounter. But a lightning right inside the first minute caught the Scot, shunting him down on his backside, and the writing was on the wall. He got to his feet – and was sent back down by another shuddering right. As he kneeled, staring at the canvas, there was no way back. He did get to his feet, but the referee refused to let the fight continue and Joshua had added the Commonwealth title to his collection in characteristically pyrotechnic style.

"There's no extra time," Joshua said after what was his 14th pro outing. "Credit to Gary where credit is due. He's a big man and had a solid jab. It's a 12-round fight and I wasn't trying to dish it all out in round one, but I managed to find shots to get the job done. I was trying to slip his long solid jabs and counter him and he went tumbling down. If I leave it and start taking my time, then it could be me on the end of those shots in five rounds' time."

AJ's final fight of 2015 was scheduled for December at the O2. Intriguingly, it saw him up against a familiar foe in the shape of Dillian Whyte, the man who had inflicted his first ever defeat on Joshua as an amateur in a pub in north London six years earlier. Whyte had turned professional in 2011, two years earlier than his old rival, and although his progress through the full-time ranks had not been spectacular, he went into the clash with an unbeaten record of 16 straight victories, 13 by knockout. If he could make it 17 and once again conquer Joshua, he would inherit his WBC and Commonwealth belts, as well as the British heavyweight title vacated by Tyson Fury.

The fight turned out to be a fascinating and at times acrimonious step into the unknown for AJ. The first round was AJ's thanks to a series of shuddering blows, and for the final minute of the opener it looked as though Whyte might not survive. The bad blood between the pair surfaced as the bell sounded when Joshua caught his old rival with a late shot. Whyte had to be held back by the referee as he tried to exact retribution, and both corners came piling into the ring in what was a brief but ugly mêlée.

Order was eventually restored. The second stanza then saw the aggressive Whyte twice catch his opponent with crunching shots that visibly hurt him. AJ was in a real fight now. The third round came and went, and for the first time in his career, Joshua was required to get up from his corner and fight in a fourth. It was time to fall back on all those countless hours of work in the gym.

Whyte continued to swing bravely and AJ was unable to put his man away. Not until midway through the seventh round did he finally deliver the coup de grâce. A big right rocked Whyte and Joshua sensed his moment, piling forward with a flurry of punches and then delivering a thunderous

8 EPIC
KLITSCHKO
BATTLE

AJ's IBF triumph had propelled him into the top of echelons of the sport, but he now had to fight one of the division's biggest beasts to prove himself a truly great heavyweight

It had taken Joshua just 16 fights and less than three years to transform himself from inexperienced professional debutant into a world champion. It was by any measure a remarkable and rapid career arc, but AJ viewed his victory over Charles Martin as the beginning of a new chapter rather than the culmination of his efforts. The 26-year-old wanted more belts.

By taking the IBF title in April 2016, he became one of three world champions at the time. The American Deontay Wilder was in possession of the WBC belt while fellow Brit Tyson Fury was the holder of the WBO, IBO and WBA versions. Both men were firmly in his sights, but the politics of boxing is nothing if not complex and he first had to defend his own title.

The man selected as the first challenger was an American named Dominic Breazeale, and the pair were scheduled to fight at the O2 in June. With an unbeaten record in his 17 professional bouts and standing at six foot seven, Breazeale seemed a daunting prospect. However, he had beaten no one of real note and many confidently predicted a comfortable evening's work for AJ in east London.

The champion did successfully defend his crown, though the clash did not quite follow the script.

The opening two rounds saw Joshua work his jab effectively, and a couple of left hooks certainly rocked the challenger from across the Atlantic. By the end of the fourth, Breazeale was sporting a swollen eye, but he was still standing. He even caught Joshua with a decent right in the fifth. Not until the seventh round was the champion finally able to make his superior power tell, catching the challenger with an explosive left that reduced him to a crumpled heap on the canvas.

BELOW: AJ
intensified his
training regime
ahead of his pivotal
clash with Wladimir
Klitschko at
Wembley Stadium,
the 19th fight of his
professional career.

determination from both men, but the pre-fight press conferences were more articulate and, as a result, more revealing than boxing fans expected.

"Boxing is a violent sport but we all can be friendly with each other," Klitschko told the media. "Respect is never going to get lost, but once that bell rings, one man needs to go down and the other needs to conquer. When the last bell rings, we will shake hands again. In between, on the night, we will be enemies. We will definitely show the world that despite the violence, we can handle each other respectfully before and after.

"This is a big step for AJ. He hasn't fought this type of quality fighter yet. It's going to be challenging for him, and it's going to be challenging for me. This fight is fifty-fifty, both fighters have a chance to win the fight, but I have this feeling that this is my night.

"I'm the challenger again. I feel young, hungry, humble and totally obsessed with my goal to raise my hands again. I'm so obsessed with winning. I realized that life is a circle, and I see myself in AJ. I do believe I know how he thinks, how he goes, and how the actual fight is going to be.

"The belts are very important. I've been attached to these belts for a very long time. The only difference is in my last fight they went to the opposite corner. So my goal and obsession is for those belts to land in my corner, in my hands. Obsession is love in extreme shape. I'm in love with my goal."

For AJ, the build-up was characterized by questions about how he would cope with the gulf in top-level experience between himself and his decorated opponent. After all, he was 14 years Klitschko's junior. What's more, with 49 fewer professional fights under his belt, he had much less ring guile.

"Let's strip it right back to what it is – a young lion, ferocious, hungry, very determined," he said. "I left no stone unturned in training camp.

Someone is going to win and someone is going to continue with their career and I'm very confident that's me.

"Even though it's an amazing event I try to strip everything back down. It's me and a man coming to blows – and the best man will win. I'm preparing physically and mentally for any battle. That's why I enjoy the sport and take it seriously. It is just another stepping stone towards greatness. I'm only going to be myself – the fight is already as big as it can be.

"There are belts on the line, there's legacy on the line, there's 12 rounds of intense, ferocious boxing on the line. It comes with everything you want to see – boxing skills, power, timing. It's just how long you can last and withstand each other's abilities."

There was nothing to choose between the two in terms of height, both men six foot six. Joshua just had the edge on the scales, weighing in at 250 pounds for the big fight against the 41-year-old Klitschko at 240.5 pounds. Neither, then, had a clear physical advantage. It would, most agreed, be a contest decided by the relative merits of AJ's youthful dynamism against the Ukrainian's battle-hardened experience.

A post-war British record of 90,000 people crammed into Wembley on 29 April 2017 for the clash. Millions more would watch in the 150 countries worldwide who televised the £30 million bout. The time had come to discover whether Joshua was the real deal.

He emerged from the famous Wembley tunnel wearing a white robe over white shorts, boots and gloves. Before entering the ring, he was hoisted aloft on a hydraulic platform to greet the cheering, partisan crowd, flanked either side by the flaming letters "A" and "J". The home of football was ready for the biggest night ever in British boxing history. Smiling and

" You can't deny it, this is epic. As much as I'm calm, when I look around and see how pumped people are for this fight, it gives me energy, it gives me life. "

JOSHUA looks ahead to the Klitschko fight

OPPOSITE: AJ's epic clash with Klitschko at Wembley was the most brutal of his career and the first time he was knocked down since turning professional.

FOLLOWING PAGES: Wladimir Klitschko is on his knees and AJ is already celebrating as referee David Fields sends him to a corner; the fight is about to end with Joshua a TKO-winner in the 11th round.

"I knew it was possible to hurt him, but I am learning round by round," he said. "I'm learning under the bright lights. I don't come to box, I come to hurt people. With all due respect, I came to hurt him. At the end of the day, I figured out what I had to do and got him done.

"There's been many a time in training when we go into the 11th round and I'm tired but I know I have to keep it up because I have to go the distance. I showed tonight that fights are won in the gym. It gets tough and boxing isn't easy. You have to have the whole package. I don't mind fighting him again, if he wants the rematch. Big respect to Wladimir for challenging the young lions of the division."

Defeat for Klitschko ended his dream of regaining the belts he'd lost to Fury in 2015. Philosophical about the result, he conceded in his post-fight interview that he had spurned his best chance of victory after knocking down AJ in the sixth round.

"I thought he wouldn't get up," he confessed. "I think I should have done more straight after he went down. But I was pretty sure it was going to be my night, so I took my time. I think Joshua and I both did great. I think we did a lot for the sport in the way we performed and how we respected and treated each other. It was a great night for boxing and the fans.

"Tonight, we all won. I didn't get the belts, but I didn't feel like I lost – not my name, my face, nor my reputation. It was great to be involved in such an amazing occasion. I have always been a fan of AJ's talent. He beat me and he won the fight, shows his qualities. The best man won and it's a massive event for boxing. Two gentlemen fought each other. Anthony was better. It's really sad I didn't make it. He is unified champion and I have to cheer up. He did what he was supposed to do."

Victory instantly catapulted AJ into the realms of global superstar. The reaction in the media in the wake of the fight was as emphatic as his destructive display in the final round at Wembley.

"From the moment the final blows of a magnificent fight rippled down Anthony Joshua's 27-year-old arms on to the bleeding and battered head of the 41-year-old Wladimir Klitschko in the 11th round, there could be no more arguments about who is the best heavyweight in the world," wrote Kevin Mitchell in *The Guardian*.

"It was not just that Joshua, unbeaten in all 19 professional fights, had added the WBA super version of the title to his own IBF belt, or even that he had stopped one of boxing's finest old champions. What secured the winner's acclaim was that he got up from a right cross in the sixth that would have felled an elephant.

"Probably unsure what city he was in, he fought on through a daze to bring the contest to the most dramatic conclusion, and will rule until someone of equal stature unseats him. There is nobody of that calibre on the horizon."

" I'm not perfect, but I'm trying and, if you don't take part, you're going to fail. Boxing is about character. There is nowhere to hide. No complications about boxing. Anyone can do this. Give it a go. You leave your ego at the door. Massive respect to Klitschko. He's a role model in and out of the ring and I've got nothing but love and respect for anyone who steps in the ring. London, I love you. Can I go home now? **"**

AJ talks to the Wembley crowd after his dramatic victory over Wladimir Klitschko

William HILL
matchroomboxing
sky sports box office
JDSPORTS.COM
StubHub
ANTHONY JOSHUA
LEONE
RIVAL

9 DEFENDING
HIS CROWN

OPPOSITE: Joshua
was expected to
defend his titles
at the Principality
Stadium against
Kubrat Pulev but the
Bulgarian pulled out
at late notice with a
shoulder injury.

His opponent, nicknamed "The Cobra", was in buoyant mood after the confirmation that he now had a second shot at a world belt. He predicted a confrontational fight – and one that he would win. "Anthony is a formidable opponent. We will not hug and hold, we will not run. We will stand and fight. His style fits mine perfectly, and in boxing, styles make fights. My preparation will be very intense, and I will be perfectly ready when I enter the ring so that he will have no chance to beat me."

Both men duly retreated to put in the hard work in the gym. Then, just 12 days before they were scheduled to meet in the Principality, it was revealed that Pulev had injured his shoulder in sparring. At the 11th hour, Cameroonian-French heavyweight Carlos Takam was drafted in as a replacement.

"I received a call from [Pulev's promoter] Kalle Sauerland to inform me that Pulev had injured his shoulder and may be ruled out of the fight – this was later confirmed by his doctor," explained Hearn. "IBF rules state that the mandatory will go to the next fighter in line, which is Carlos Takam.

"When the Pulev fight was announced I made a deal with Takam's team to begin camp and be on standby for this fight. When I called them, they were overjoyed and good to go. It's a difficult position for AJ. Having prepared meticulously for the style and height of Pulev, he now faces a completely different style and challenge in Takam. This hasn't happened in his career before, but he is ready for all comers."

The physical contrast between Pulev and Takam was undeniably stark. Two-and-a-half inches shorter than the injured Bulgarian, the new challenger was an altogether stockier and more muscular opponent for the champion. Although he had not previously boxed for a world title, he had represented Cameroon at the 2004 Olympics, and in 35 pro fights, he had been beaten only three times. One of those three defeats came in May 2016, when he took New Zealand's Joseph Parker 12 rounds in Auckland. It was testament to his pedigree that just seven months later Parker was crowned WBO world champion.

The late change in fighters was far from ideal for Joshua, who had celebrated his 28th birthday earlier in the month. Now facing a very different tactical and physical challenge in the form of Takam, he had precious little time to adjust his training regime in the build-up to the first defence of his three titles. It was not a change that seemed to unduly unsettle the defending champion.

"Believe it or not, I still have the mindset of a challenger. I don't walk around with an ego just because I have a few belts on my shoulder. I know he has that mindset to find a way to win. If you keep on knocking on the door, you find a way through. I just have to boot him out because he isn't coming through this door.

"I'm still developing. I think that's why people jump at the opportunity. If I trash-talked more, I may be more feared. But my job is to break them

sky sports box office
matchroomboxing
William HILL
RIVAL
ANTHONY
sky sports box office
William HILL
William HILL
sky sports box office
matchroomboxing

ANTHONY
William HILL
TAKAM
JOSHUA
matchroomboxing
sky sports
box office

though he was still unable to put his man away. For only the second time in his career, Joshua was heading into a 10th round.

Takam's heroic resistance undoubtedly endeared him to the Cardiff crowd, but his fairytale finally came to an end midway through the tenth. Two big lefts from the champion piled on the pressure and as AJ surged forward, the battered and bruised challenger could no longer summon the energy to fire anything back at him. The referee came between the two fighters. Joshua had successfully defended his WBA, IBF and IBO world heavyweight titles – but he had been made to work harder than anticipated.

The decision to stop the contest was greeted by jeers in certain sections of the crowd. Their displeasure, though, was aimed at neither the champion nor Takam. The fans were simply upset not to see such an epic encounter go the full distance. Given the damage the challenger had sustained, it was probably the right decision.

Takam begged to differ. "I don't know why the referee stopped the match. I respect the champion and the UK fans, they are great fans and I am happy to box here, but I don't know why they stopped it. I want a rematch. I make my preparations with 12 days to fight Anthony and I want to box him again."

Joshua admitted he was ultimately a relieved man to get his first multiple title defence out of the way. He refused to become embroiled in the debate over the referee's decision and insisted his main concern was getting the fight finished despite struggling with his broken nose.

"I come to fight. I don't sit on the edge and make decisions. It was a good fight until the ref stopped it, so I have the utmost respect for Takam. I have no interest in what's going on with the officials. That's not my job. My job is to worry about my opponent. I was watching him. I was trying to take him down round by round and unfortunately the ref stopped it before.

"I couldn't breathe [because of his nose]. He started catching up in the later rounds and it would've been a massive disaster, so I had to keep my cool. I have a couple of months to heel it up. I'm going to see some good doctors to crack it back into place."

Reaction to AJ's triumph was not quite as euphoric as it had been six months earlier when he defeated Klitschko. Even so, there was widespread agreement that his win was just the beginning of a long reign as the unified, and potentially in the future undisputed, world heavyweight champion.

"Joshua had thrown everything at the super-sub with the tank-like physique and granite chin, but he was beginning to tire when Edwards stepped in to bring the fight to a close, much to Takam's fury," wrote Gareth A. Davies in the *Daily Telegraph*. "At the end of it all the young man who is fast becoming a superstar now has a record which reads 20 fights, 20 stoppages.

"But Takam proved a tough man to put down, with Joshua only able to put him away in the 10th when Edwards felt Takam had taken enough punishment after a right nearly knocked him off his feet. It seemed premature, but Joshua's bandwagon goes marching on."

" This was just the type of fight, experience and adversity that Anthony Joshua needed. He wasn't at his best, but you won't always be and it's those times you have to find a way. Some fall apart after a broken nose, but he remained composed and controlled the fight. It would have been nice just to let it play out one way or another because Takam still looked strong. It was a very good test for AJ, though, especially with the broken nose. "

LENNOX LEWIS, former undisputed world heavyweight champion, on Joshua's victory over Carlos Takam

Joshua's work for 2017 was done, but in January the next chapter in his career became clearer when it was announced his 21st and most seminal fight yet would be against New Zealand's unbeaten Joseph Parker at the end of March. AJ would return to Cardiff and the Principality Stadium for the bout and this time it was not only Joshua's titles that would be on the line.

Victorious in all 24 of his pro fights, Parker had claimed the WBO heavyweight belt by beating American Andy Ruiz in Auckland in December 2016. He had twice successfully defended his crown before the confirmation he would cross swords with AJ, and that meant their

Principality showdown would be a unification fight for three of the division's four biggest belts. It would be the first time in history two reigning heavyweight champions had met in Britain and also the first time since 1987, when Mike Tyson outpointed Tony Tucker in Las Vegas, that two unbeaten heavyweight champions had stepped into the ring together.

The build-up to the clash saw AJ installed as the firm favourite to extend his unbeaten record, but with Parker boasting 18 knockouts in his 24 fights, Joshua was under no illusions; his Kiwi opponent represented a genuine threat to his status as the division's top dog.

OPPOSITE: Joshua became a triple world champion in Cardiff but, for the first time in his career, he was taken the distance by his opponent.

"People should never overlook Joseph Parker," he said. "He's a world champion, undefeated, and he has that Kiwi blood. That's a triple threat. I'm taking this deadly serious, and I'm focused on the task ahead.

"Anyone I fight, they always come 30 per cent better than what I've seen so I can't expect the same old Parker in the ring. That's where my goal is and that's where I'm focused on. I can't take my eye off this guy. He's talented and he wants to prove himself."

Joshua weighed in at 17 stone and four pounds for the fight, almost a stone lighter than he had been for his clash with Takam, but he was still heavier than his Kiwi opponent and with a significant height and reach advantage, the champion looked supremely prepared for the challenge ahead.

A boisterous crowd of 78,000 inside the Principality Stadium were on their feet when AJ emerged from the dressing room, and the fight that unfolded in front of them was as engrossing as it was tactical as the two men in the ring both showed their quality, resolve and durability.

AJ's left jab ensured Parker was rarely allowed inside his defences to unload from close range, but the challenger was unperturbed as he repeatedly came forward looking for an opening. Joshua's respect for his opponent was obvious and although he was ahead on the scorecards from the opening round, the home favourite resisted the temptation to gamble everything on a decisive assault.

Two big left hooks from the champion in the 10th gave the crowd reason to cheer, only for Parker to connect with a good shot of his own in the eleventh, but there was to be no early conclusion to proceedings and for the first time in his career, AJ was taken the full 12 rounds.

The judges would decide the winner but there was no real doubt Joshua was the victor and the scorecards, reading 118-110, 118-110 and 119-109 in his favour, confirmed his superiority on the night. AJ was now the unified WBA, IBF and WBO world heavyweight champion.

"There's a lot more to come," he said after his twenty-first straight win since turning professional. "We have to roll with the punches. I am developing. My amateur career was three-and-a-half years. This October is five years as a pro. In boxing I have always put my heart on my sleeve and showed the world good and bad. I will always be honest, give you who I am and my best. Everyone will enjoy this journey and you'll see the good, bad and ugly. If I can keep controlling fighters like that, I will be about a long time."

It was not in truth the most pyrotechnic performance of his career, but it did reflect the champion's growing maturity. "I thought it was an assured performance from Joshua," wrote the BBC's boxing correspondent Mike Costello. "He clearly thought early on that he may be going the distance and adjusted his pace to suit. We also have to consider that Parker for long periods, as game and as resilient as he was, appeared to be in damage limitation mode."

" I knew how to break him down and put him in a position so he couldn't give much back. Every time he came forward I just rammed that jab in his face. We've always been in at the deep end with high expectations. I just focus on improving. I know the expectations of what I can achieve are very possible but without dedication they won't happen. The sky is the limit. I'm not elated because I don't let the highs get to my head. We have to go again soon. **"**

AJ looks ahead after victory over Joseph Parker in Cardiff

10 | **WHAT NEXT**
FOR AJ?

WHAT NEXT FOR AJ?

The future is bright for Britain's triple heavyweight world champion both in and out of the ring as he strives to cement his reputation as one of boxing's greatest ever fighters

Victory over Joseph Parker in Cardiff underlined AJ's status as the best heavyweight on the planet, but the WBC belt held by American Deontay Wilder still eluded him.

In the three-decade-long era of heavyweight boxing's quartet of major titles – the WBA, IBF, WBO and WBC – no fighter has ever laid claim to all four belts simultaneously. AJ's triumph in Cardiff meant he was now in possession of three of the four and one tantalizing step closer to achieving the Holy Grail of becoming the division's first man to hold the quartet at the same time.

Unsurprisingly Wilder's name was on everyone's lips inside the Principality Stadium from the moment the judges confirmed Joshua had outpointed Parker. The American had successfully defended his WBC title for the seventh time earlier in March, stopping Cuban Luis Ortiz in the 10th round in New York City, and even as AJ celebrated inside the ring, fans were calling for confirmation of a winner-takes-all fight that pundits agreed would smash box office records.

Wilder had turned down an invitation to watch Joshua fight Parker in Wales but despite his absence, AJ was quick to challenge the bronze medallist from the 2008 Beijing Olympics to go head-to-head.

"Are you asking me if I want to become undisputed champion of the world?" he said. "IBO, IBF, WBA, WBO – 21 professional fights, six world title fights. Does that not show how good I'm going? Forget the hype, I'm about business, let's get the business done. What would I have to do to beat Wilder? Get him in the ring and I knock him spark out."

The potential location of the fight proved a potential stumbling block, however, with Joshua insisting the American would have to come to the UK while Wilder was insistent the champion would have to defend his

three belts on the other side of the Atlantic in what would be AJ's first professional fight abroad.

"Everybody wants to see the fight," Wilder said. "The only people that don't are his promoters. They already know how big of a risk this really is. They should be worried but how long do they really think the public, the fans of boxing are going to allow them to stay away from me? This is the biggest fight in our era.

"Does he want to be remembered as a country-wide champion? Because he's not worldwide. Over here in America they don't even know his name. They just know him as a big guy from England. I need him and he needs me at the end of the day, unless he doesn't want to unify. Unless he wants to stay over his side of the pond and let people gravitate to him."

Whatever unfolds in the future inside the ring, Joshua will continue to be a busy man outside it, and he has made no secret that when the day does come to hang up his gloves he will be happy to swap the gym for the boardroom as he continues to build his business empire.

He took his significant first step towards this in 2015 when he set up "AJ Boxing and Commercial" to manage his sponsorship contracts and merchandise range. His blue chip sponsors include Jaguar Land Rover, Under Armour, Beats by Dre and Vodafone – and his relationship with these companies is all part of his ambitious plans for the future.

"When I first started boxing, the aim was to become a multimillionaire," he said in an interview with *GQ* magazine. "But now there are ordinary people, grandmas and granddads, who are worth millions just because of property prices. So the new school of thought is that I need to be a billionaire. Being a millionaire is good, but you have to set your sights higher. If I'm making £10 million from my next fight, my next target has to be making ten times that. And if I get to £100m–150m, why not go for the billion? I know self-made billionaires. It's hard, but it's possible."

Another arm to "AJ Boxing and Commercial" is the company's athlete management activities, and with the lure of working with Joshua, the department has already signed up two of British boxing's rising stars – 2016 Olympic light heavyweight champion Joshua Buatsi and unbeaten cruiserweight Lawrence Okolie, another of Team GB's fighters at the Rio Games.

AJ is also a shareholder in the exclusive BXR Gym in London, where he sometimes trains, and with his branded merchandise proving more popular with each fight, his business interests are going from strength to strength.

The combative nature of all successful boxers is part of AJ's DNA and in the build-up to the Parker fight, he admitted he could one day be tempted to swap the ring for the cage and try his hand at mixed martial arts.

"Providing I've got to the end of my career and achieved what I wanted to. Since the question was asked, I said, 'Yes, it would be an option because it's been done before and it's successful.' So it can be done again. I have to complete the goals and achievements I have in boxing otherwise it's like a pantomime. You have to dominate your own sport, and then you can look at other avenues."

Joshua's personal life looks certain to be equally frenetic going forward. He became a father to Joseph Bayley Temiloluwa Prince Joshua in late 2015 – born at Watford General Hospital – and he has admitted that fatherhood has given him a different perspective on the future.

"Before it was all about me," he said. "When he was born I thought I don't want to change because I'm very regimented but it's been a blessing. I lived for myself but then when I had my son, I started realizing there is someone who is going to be here after I'm gone and that's what he taught me, build something that they will respect and appreciate when I'm not here any more."

FOLLOWING PAGES: Deontay Wilder's victory over Luis Ortiz in New York in March 2018 put the WBC champion on a collision course with AJ.

" I want to be the undisputed champion of the world. I do understand now, I have to play the game, if I want to create a legacy. I think I understand now, everything I have to gain and everything I have to do. I've never played a role. But look at the likes of Muhammad Ali, who became a sporting icon. Before I was happy to just be a part of boxing, and felt wherever I get to, it was always better than where I started. I never had a minute to reflect. But now I want to stamp my mark and my legacy and be among the likes of Federer. If I want to be considered like these guys, I have to carry myself the right way. I want to be like the Ronaldos, Messis and Federers. That's where I want to take boxing. **"**

CAREER
STATISTICS

Date	Venue	Opponent	Result	Details	Notes
20-Mar-10	London	Luke Herdman (GB)	Win	2nd-round stoppage	English ABA Elite National Championships
17-Apr-10	Bideford	Chris Duff (GB)	Win	Walkover	English ABA Elite National Championships
2-May-10	King's Lynn	Simon Hadden (GB)	Win	Walkover	English ABA Elite National Championships
14-May-10	London	Dominic Winrow (GB)	Win	1st-round stoppage	English ABA Elite National Championships
20-Jun-10	Alexandra Palace, London	Otto Wallin (SE)	Win	Points	Haringey Box Cup
30-Oct-10	Aldershot	Chris Devanney (IE)	Win	2nd-round stoppage	England v Ireland International
13-Nov-10	Manchester	Amin Isa (GB)	Win	Points 6:3	GB Amateur Boxing Championships
8-Dec-10	Wesport	Chris Turner (IE)	Win	Points 6:3	Ireland v England International
14-Jan-11	Stockholm	Otto Wallin (SE)	Win	Points 3:0	Sweden v England International
13-May-11	Colchester	Fayz Aboadi Abbas (GB)	Win	Points 24:15	English ABA Elite National Championships
18-Jun-11	Ankara, TR	Eric Brechlin (DE)	Win	Points 23:16	European Amateur Boxing Championships
20-Jun-11	Ankara, TR	Cathal McMonagle (IE)	Win	Points 22:10	European Amateur Boxing Championships

Despite a couple of rare blemishes, AJ's globe-trotting amateur career saw him rack up dozens of impressive performances. He quickly established himself as one of the most exciting young fighters on the scene

Date	Venue	Opponent	Result	Details	Notes
21-Jun-11	Ankara, TR	Mihai Nistor (RO)	Loss	3rd-round stoppage	European Amateur Boxing Championships
29-Sep-11	Baku, AZ	Tariq Abdul-Haqq (TT)	Win	3rd-round stoppage	AIBA World Boxing Championships
2-Oct-11	Baku, AZ	Juan Isidro Hiracheta (MX)	Win	1st-round stoppage	AIBA World Boxing Championships
4-Oct-11	Baku, AZ	Mohamed Arjaoui (MA)	Win	Points 16:7	AIBA World Boxing Championships
5-Oct-11	Baku, AZ	Roberto Cammarelle (IT)	Win	Points: 15:13	AIBA World Boxing Championships
7-Oct-11	Baku, AZ	Erik Pfeiffer (DE)	Win	1st-round stoppage	AIBA World Boxing Championships
8-Oct-11	Baku, AZ	Magomedrasul Medzhidov (AZ)	Loss	Points 21:22	AIBA World Boxing Championships
10-Feb-12	Debrecen, HUN	Sergey Kuzmin (RU)	Win	Points 9:7	Bocskai Memorial Tournament
11-Feb-12	Debrecen, HUN	Sardor Abdullayev (UZ)	Win	3rd-round stoppage	Bocskai Memorial Tournament
10-May-12	Kaunas, LTU	Sean Turner (IE)	Win	Points 9:5	Algirdas Socikas Tournament
11-May-12	Kaunas, LTU	Johan Linde (AT)	Win	1st-round knockout	Algirdas Socikas Tournament
12-May-12	Kaunas, LTU	Aidas Petruskevicius (LT)	Win	Walkover	Algirdas Socikas Tournament

Date	Venue	Opponent	Result	Details
1-Aug-12	Excel, London	Erislandy Savon (CU)	Win	Points 17:16
6-Aug-12	Excel, London	Zhang Zhilei (CN)	Win	Points 15:11
10-Aug-12	Excel, London	Ivan Dychko (KZ)	Win	Points 13:11
12-Aug-12	Excel, London	Roberto Cammarelle (IT)	Win	Points 18:18 (count back)

Date	Venue	Opponent	Result	Details
5-Oct-13	O2 Arena, London	Emanuele Leo (IT)	Win	1st-round stoppage
26-Oct-13	Motorpoint Arena, Sheffield	Paul Butlin (GB)	Win	2nd-round stoppage
14-Nov-13	York Hall, London	Hrvoje Kisicek (HR)	Win	2nd-round stoppage
1-Feb-14	Motorpoint Arena, Cardiff	Dorian Darch (GB)	Win	2nd-round stoppage

Turning pro did nothing to slow Joshua's ascent – as the numbers show with brutal clarity. The question wasn't whether AJ was ready to take on the world, it was whether the world was ready for him

Date	Venue	Opponent	Result	Details
1-Mar-14	SEEC, Glasgow	Hector Avila (AR)	Win	1st-round knockout
31-May-14	Wembley Stadium, London	Matt Legg (GB)	Win	1st-round knockout
12-Jul-14	Echo Arena, Liverpool	Matt Skelton (GB)	Win	2nd-round stoppage
13-Sep-14	Phones 4U Arena, Manchester	Konstantin Airich (DE)	Win	3rd-round stoppage

CHAMPIONSHIP STATISTICS

Date	Venue	Opponent	Result	Details	Notes
11-Oct-14	O2 Arena, London	Denis Bakhtov (RU)	Win	2nd-round stoppage	Won vacant WBC International heavyweight title
22-Nov-14	Echo Arena, Liverpool	Michael Sprott (GB)	Win	1st-round stoppage	
4-Apr-15	Metro Radio Arena, Newcastle	Jason Gavern (US)	Win	3rd-round stoppage	
9-May-15	Barclaycard Arena, Birmingham	Raphael Zumbano Love (BR)	Win	2nd-round stoppage	
30-May-15	O2 Arena, London	Kevin Johnson (US)	Win	2nd-round stoppage	Retained WBC International heavyweight title
12-Sep-15	O2 Arena, London	Gary Cornish (GB)	Win	1st-round stoppage	Retained WBC International heavyweight title; won vacant Commonwealth heavyweight title
12-Dec-15	O2 Arena, London	Dillian Whyte (GB)	Win	7th-round knockout	Retained WBC International and Commonwealth heavyweight titles; won vacant British heavyweight title
9-Apr-16	O2 Arena, London	Charles Martin (US)	Win	2nd-round knockout	Won vacant IBF heavyweight title
25-Jun-16	O2 Arena, London	Dominic Breazeale (US)	Win	7th-round stoppage	Retained IBF heavyweight title
10-Dec-16	Manchester Arena	Eric Molina (US)	Win	3rd-round stoppage	Retained IBF heavyweight title
29-Apr-17	Wembley Stadium, London	Wladimir Klitschko (UA)	Win	11th-round stoppage	Retained vacant IBF heavyweight title; win vacant WBA (Super) and IBO heavyweight titles
28-Oct-17	Principality Stadium, Cardiff	Carlos Takam (FR)	Win	10th-round stoppage	Retained WBA (Super), IBF and IBO heavyweight titles
31-Mar-18	Principality Stadium, Cardiff	Joseph Parker (NZ)	Win	Unanimous points decision	Retained WBA (Super), IBF and IBO heavyweight titles, won WBO heavyweight title

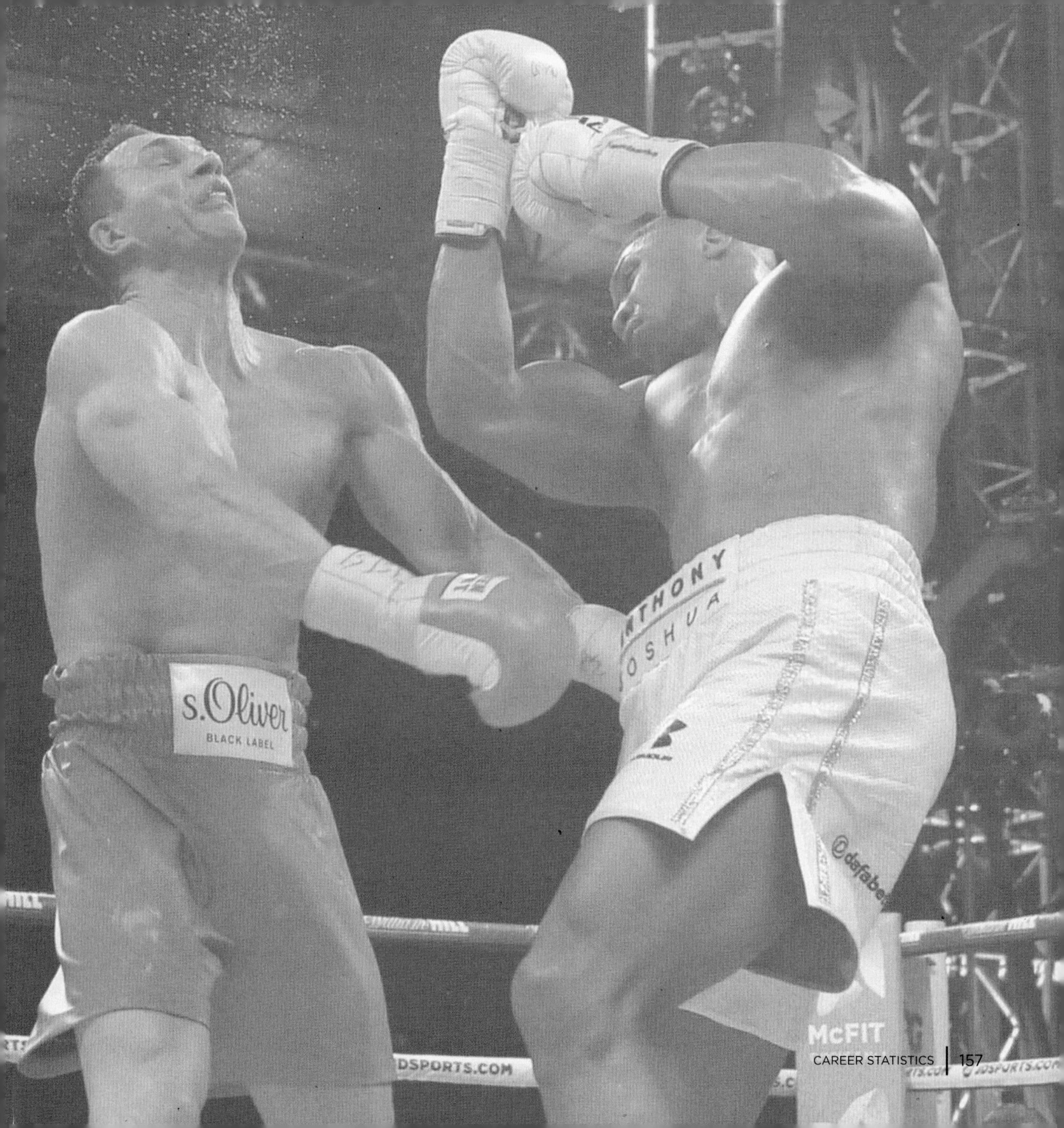
s.Oliver
BLACK LABEL
McFIT

The publishers would like to thank the following sources for their kind permission to reproduce the pictures in this book.

Alamy: /Action Plus Sports Images: 80; /DPA Picture Alliance: 82, 115; /HFP Images: 118-119, 124, 130; /Scott Heavey: 9, 12-13, 107, 148-149; /Sport In Pictures: 35; /Adina Tovy: 50

Getty Images: 28, 31; /David M Benett: 142; /Charlie Crowhurst: 18BL; /Edward Diller/Icon Sportswire: 144-145; /Julian Finney: 135; /Stu Forster: 121; /John Gichigi: 18TR; /Richard Heathcote: 6-7, 11, 15, 104-105, 116, 123, 132, 136, 138-139, 141, 146, 156-157, 158-159; / Scott Heavey: 18TL, 54, 56, 58-59, 63, 65, 66-67, 69, 87, 88; /Dave J Hogan: 72; /Tom Jenkins: 96-97; / Stephen McCarthy/Sportsfile: 4; / Dan Mullan: 110; /Clive Rose: 37; / Mark Runnacles: 77; /Paul Thomas: 74-75, 81, 154-155; /Visionhaus/ Corbis: 2

REX/Shutterstock: 53; / Graham Chadwick: 32-33, 78; / Zsolt Czegledi/EPA: 27; /Alan Davidson/Silverhub: 36; /Matt Dunham/AP: 90-91, 102, 108; / Gareth Everett/Huw Evans: 129; /Chris Fairweather/Huw Evans: 126-127; /David Fisher: 62; / Paul Grover: 44; /Scott Heavey/ BPI: 46-47, 95; /Andy Hooper/ Associated Newspapers: 85; / Huw Evans Agency: 70; /Osman Karimov/AP: 20-21, 24, 150-151; /James Marsh/BPI: 112; / Geoff Pugh: 49; /Kevin Quigley/ Associated Newspapers: 61, 93, 100; /Dan Rowley: 43; /Dennis M Sabangan/EPA: 40-41; /Patrick Semansky/AP: 152-153; /Dave Shopland/BPI: 133; /Larry W Smith/EPA: 39; /TGSPhoto: 18BR; /Michael Zemanek/BPI: 99

Every effort has been made to acknowledge correctly and contact the source and/or copyright holder of each picture and Carlton Books Limited apologises for any unintentional errors or omissions, which will be, corrected in future editions of this book.